MOTHER DAUGHTER JOURNAL

by Katie Clemons

https://katieclemons.com
#celebratemystory

To Maureen and Michelle,
who share the beauty of being
a daughter, sister, and mom with me.

Gadanke
PO Box 812
Livingston, MT
59047 USA

Design and text by Katie Clemons.
Copyright ©2016 Katie Clemons LLC.
Published in the United States by Katie Clemons LLC.

https://gadanke.com
Printed in USA

ISBN: 978-1-63336-002-0
Edition 1.1

A Mom's Perspective

"Katie, what are you still doing in the bathroom?"

I swear my mom always knew when trouble was brewing. One of my best lessons came when I was about eleven years old.

"I'm not doing anything, Mom!" I shot back, frantically scooping up the confetti of hair clippings on the sink. I couldn't see a safe place to hide my evidence, so I tossed the blonde wad into the toilet and flushed.

"That doesn't sound like nothing."

I looked in the mirror and grimaced. So far, my new bangs—which were supposed to look adorable and bouncy like the model in the picture—resembled something a weed wacker might cough out. My friends were going to laugh; my brother and his cute buddies would tease me; and I'd never be able to leave home again. The harder I tried to fix my hair, the shorter and more ridiculous it became.

My mom leaned into the door and asked, "Are you okay in there? If you have anything you want to talk about, I'm right here."

"You don't get it, Mom. Everything's fine," I answered, trying not to do that choking-sob thing. I jerked the medicine cabinet open and scanned the contents while tears blurred my vision. "I'm just trying out that new face wash you bought me."

Anyone else in the family wouldn't have given two seconds' notice to my tone. They'd have banged on the door to use the toilet or snoop around. But for whatever reason, my mom didn't push. She just said "Okay" and returned to the living room.

Now that I'm a mom, I know how difficult it was for her to walk away. When my child is in distress, my primal reaction is to bust down the door and announce: "Let's talk about this right now. I'll fix everything!" I get so wrapped up in my own need to restore happiness that I forget: sometimes my child needs to learn how to overcome adversity without me.

I and other moms have found that keeping a journal helps us become both more aware and confident. Our hectic schedules make it easy to unintentionally walk through the hall and completely miss a child's closed door, while writing prompts usher us to slow down and be more aware of what our children—and we!—are experiencing. It's like watching clouds. Once we let ourselves lean into the grass, clouds start transforming from cotton balls in the sky to shapes and stories that dance and shift. We start seeing connections. You might see one story in the clouds; your daughter—looking through her lens of adolescence and varying life experiences—sees something different. Mother-daughter journaling lends you both the opportunity to recognize similarities and differences while openly discussing them.

I still remember searching for my mom that long-ago summer afternoon. She was sitting on a red and white gingham quilt spread across the lawn, sipping iced tea. "I did something bad," I told her. She just patted the quilt beside her, inviting me to sit. I pulled the baseball cap off my head and showed her the porcupine my bangs had become. I wanted to cry all over again.

She set her tea down and smiled. "You know, I've been trying new things my whole life too. You never know what will happen if you don't pull out scissors and try."

Although I never shared a journal with my mom, moments like these are threads that connect me forever with her love. I wrote this journal to encourage you and your daughter to share stories, daydreams, adventures, and to try and understand each other's point of view. A few prompts invite conversations on topics that may be difficult but will bring you closer together.

You'll find three types of prompts woven throughout this journal. Invite your daughter to answer them with you while you chat, or pass the book back and forth, making entries in turn. Her stories go on pages that begin "Dear Daughter" or "Daughter Writes." Corresponding "Dear Mom" and "Mom Writes" pages offer you an opportunity to respond or ignite another conversation.

Your storycatching experience only begins with this journal. Join me for special *Love, Mom and Me* resources.

Exclusively for you

https://katieclemons.com/a/R2zM

This secret link at katieclemons.com includes creative ideas for the inside covers of your journal, printable pockets to tuck in keepsakes, embellishing techniques, tips to engage your daughter, and crafty mother-daughter challenges. Enjoy watching my TEDxTalk on the power of story and subscribe to my newsletter to receive bite-sized journal keeping tips in your inbox. I call them love letters. I hope you also email me at howdy@gadanke.com (I answer all my emails) or join me on social media @gadanke.

The stories you and your daughter share in this journal capture present day conversations and create a keepsake of the past, a launchpad for the future. Imagine reading this journal in ten or twenty years: pages filled with stories and perspectives, photographs, smudges of colorful pens and glitter, youthful penmanship recording phrases you haven't heard in years, and best of all . . . reminders of how much you love each other.

Celebrate your story. It's beautiful.

I'll see you beneath the clouds.

♡ Katie

Celebrate your story.

PICTURE OF US
together

Our full names are

We call each other

We sign our names like this

We are _____ and _____ years old.

Date _____

You & Me
○ ○ ○ ○ ○ ○ ○

❶ Is this journal top secret or can anyone else know we're keeping it?

❷ Do we have to fill out the pages in numerical order?

❑ *Yes*

❑ *No*

❸ How much time do we get to write?

❹ How do we pass our journal back and forth?

5 How do we tell each other which page to turn to?

6 How do we tell each other when we need an urgent response?

7 Are there any other guidelines we should establish?

Date _____

DEAR Mom,

What's something I do that makes you smile?

DEAR Daughter,

What's something I do that makes you smile?

Date _____

YOU & ME

MOVIE WE WATCH OVER AND OVER

MOM

DAUGHTER

OUTFIT WE WEAR CONSTANTLY

MOM

DAUGHTER

DESSERT WE ALWAYS LOVE

MOM

DAUGHTER

Date _____

Tell me about a time when you did something kind
for someone else even though you didn't have to.

Why did you do it?

How did it make you feel?

Date _____

DEAR Mom,

What are your thoughts on kindness?

Do you have a story about when you saw me being nice?

Date _____ 18

DEAR *Daughter,*

Which school subject is difficult for you?

Why do you think it feels so challenging?

How can I help make it easier?

Date _____

DEAR Mom,

What do you think about what I wrote?

Which subject did you struggle with
when you were my age?

How does knowing that subject help you now?

Date _____

3 *Things* THAT MAKE US LAUGH OUT LOUD

MOM

DAUGHTER

Date _____

DEAR Mom,

Tell me what your life was like
when you were my age.

DEAR Daughter

How is your life different
and similar to when I was a kid?

Date _____

My typical weekday

6:00 _____

7:00 _____

8:00 _____

9:00 _____

10:00 _____

11:00 _____

NOON _____

1:00 _____

2:00 _____

3:00 _____

4:00 _____

5:00 _____

6:00 _____

7:00 _____

8:00 _____

9:00 _____

10:00 _____

Date _____   24

Daughter Writes

My typical weekday

6:00 _____

7:00 _____

8:00 _____

9:00 _____

10:00 _____

11:00 _____

NOON _____

1:00 _____

2:00 _____

3:00 _____

4:00 _____

5:00 _____

6:00 _____

7:00 _____

8:00 _____

9:00 _____

10:00 _____

Date _____

How did your family celebrate the holidays when you were growing up?

DEAR Daughter,

What do you love about
how our family celebrates the holidays?

Date _____

YOU & ME

RIGHT NOW WE'RE SINGING

MOM

DAUGHTER

WE'RE READING

MOM

DAUGHTER

WE'RE LOOKING FORWARD TO

MOM

DAUGHTER

Date _____

DEAR Daughter,

What are three of your most amazing accomplishments?

1 _____

_____

_____

_____

2 _____

_____

_____

_____

3 _____

_____

_____

_____

Is there another goal you want to achieve?

_____

_____

_____

Date _____

DEAR Mom,

What are your thoughts
on what I wrote about my achievements?

Do you think I can accomplish my goal?

DEAR Daughter

Why do you enjoy spending time with your friends?

Which traits do you value in a friend?

How do you try to be a good friend?

Date _____

DEAR Mom,

Why do you enjoy spending time with your friends?

Which traits do you value in a friend?

How do you try to be a good friend?

YOU & ME

THE BRAVEST WOMAN WE KNOW

MOM

DAUGHTER

THE MOST COMPASSIONATE WOMAN WE KNOW

MOM

DAUGHTER

THE HAPPIEST WOMAN WE KNOW

MOM

DAUGHTER

33

Date _____

Daughter, you are beautiful inside and out because

1 _____

_____

_____

2 _____

_____

_____

3 _____

_____

_____

I know you're intelligent because

1 _____

_____

_____

2 _____

_____

_____

HERE'S A PICTURE OF
my beautiful girl

Date _____

Mom, you are beautiful inside and out because

1 _____

_____

_____

2 _____

_____

_____

3 _____

_____

_____

I know you're intelligent because

1 _____

_____

_____

2 _____

_____

_____

HERE'S A PICTURE OF
my beautiful mom

Date _____

DEAR Mom,

Tell me about a special gift I made
for you when I was younger.

Do you still have it?

DEAR Daughter,

What do you like to make now?

Date _____

DEAR Mom,

Tell me about
the first time you held me.

DEAR Daughter,

What are four things you wish you could do?

1 _____

_____

_____

_____

2 _____

_____

_____

_____

3 _____

_____

_____

_____

4 _____

_____

_____

_____

Date _____

DEAR Mom,

What do you think about the four things I wrote?

Is there something you wish you could do?

DEAR Daughter,

I have a question
I want to ask you:

_____

_____

Date _____

DEAR Mom,

Tell me how you celebrated your birthday
when you were a kid.

What's one of your favorite birthday memories?

DEAR Daughter,

Describe how we celebrate your birthday.

Which tradition do you love most?

Tell me a favorite birthday memory.

IF I HAD A WHOLE DAY TO HAVE FUN WITH YOU

MOM

DAUGHTER

You & Me

OUR HAPPY FACES

MOM

DAUGHTER

OUR CRANKY FACES

MOM

DAUGHTER

OUR SILLY FACES

MOM

DAUGHTER

47

Date _____

DEAR Mom,

Who did you admire when you were young?

Who inspires you today?

Why is it important to have people you look up to?

DEAR Daughter

Who inspires you?

How are you similar to that person?

How can you be more like that person?

Date _____

DEAR Mom,

How do you know I love you so much?

DEAR Daughter

How do you know I love you so much?

Date _____

Mom,

OUR FAMILY

OUR TOWN

OUR HOME

OUR DINNER TABLE

Date _____

Daughter

OUR FAMILY

OUR TOWN

OUR HOME

OUR DINNER TABLE

53

Date _____

DEAR *Mom,*

What are three of your most amazing accomplishments?

1 _____

_____

_____

_____

2 _____

_____

_____

_____

3 _____

_____

_____

_____

Is there another goal you want to achieve?

_____

_____

_____

_____

Date _____

DEAR Daughter,

What do you think about the achievements I recorded?

Do you think I can accomplish my goal?

Date _____

DEAR Mom,

Tell me about
an older relative
I didn't get to know well.

5 things THAT MAKE US GRIN

MOM

DAUGHTER

Date _____

Daughter, I admire these traits in you

❶ _____

_____

_____

_____

❷ _____

_____

_____

_____

❸ _____

_____

_____

_____

❹ _____

_____

_____

_____

_____

Date _____   58

Mom, I admire these traits in you

❶ _____

_____

_____

_____

❷ _____

_____

_____

_____

❸ _____

_____

_____

_____

❹ _____

_____

_____

_____

_____

Date _____

DEAR Mom,

What are some of your favorite parts
of being a mom?

DEAR Daughter,

What do you think about what I wrote on motherhood?

Do you think you want to be a parent some day?

Date _____

WONDERFUL THINGS WE'VE DONE THIS YEAR TOGETHER

❶ _____

_____

_____

_____

❷ _____

_____

_____

_____

❸ _____

_____

_____

_____

❹ _____

_____

_____

❺ _____

_____

_____

EXCITING THINGS
WE STILL NEED TO DO
TOGETHER

❶ _____
_____
_____
_____

❷ _____
_____
_____
_____

❸ _____
_____
_____
_____

❹ _____
_____
_____

❺ _____
_____
_____

Date _____

Do you have questions about becoming a woman?

What are you excited about?

Is there anything you feel nervous about?

How do you feel about your body right now?

When do you feel confident about your body?

Do you ever feel uncomfortable about your appearance?

Date _____

What do you think about what I wrote?

Have you ever felt uncomfortable about your body?

When do you feel confident about your body?

Do you have any suggestions to help me
feel more comfortable or confident?

Tell me what you love about being a woman.

Date _____

You & Me

OUR FAVORITE DRINKS

MOM

DAUGHTER

OUR MOST DREADED CHORE

MOM

DAUGHTER

OUR TASTIEST WEEKDAY LUNCH

MOM

DAUGHTER

Date _____

DEAR Daughter,

What sport do you enjoy?

What do you like about it?

How do you feel when you're doing it?

Date _____

DEAR Mom,

What are your thoughts on sports
and what I just wrote?

Did you do any sports when you were my age?

Did you enjoy them?

DEAR Daughter,

Is there anything you wish you could change
about yourself or your life?

What would you never change?

71

DEAR Mom,

When you were my age,
what did you want to change about yourself?

Did you do anything about it?

How do you feel about it now?

Mom WRITES

Daughter, I always hear you say these expressions

1 _____

_____

_____

2 _____

_____

_____

Daughter WRITES

Mom, I always hear you say these expressions

1 _____

_____

_____

2 _____

_____

_____

Date _____

Daughter, I'm proud of you because

I admire how hard you work at

I know you're happy when

You're really good at

You regularly take time to

You make me feel loved when

You have taught me

The last thing you say to me before bed is

Date _____

Daughter WRITES

Mom, I'm proud of you because

I admire how hard you work at

I know you're happy when

You're really good at

You regularly take time to

You make me feel loved when

You have taught me

The last thing you say to me before bed is

Date _____

DEAR Mom,

Tell me a story about when I was little.

DEAR Daughter

Do you remember a story from when you were little?

Date _____

Doing something we love together

DEAR Daughter

What hobby do you enjoy?

How did you get interested in it?

What do you enjoy about it?

What's challenging?

Date _____

DEAR Mom,

What hobby do you enjoy?

How did you get interested in it?

What do you like about it?

What's challenging right now?

Best way to spend Friday night

MOM

DAUGHTER

Date _____

DEAR Mom,

What was your favorite job before I was born?

How old were you?

How did you travel to work?

What was your responsibility?

How much did you get paid?

Why did you like the job?

Did you ever make mistakes?

Do skills you learned in that job help you today?

Date _____

DEAR *Daughter,*

What do you think about my favorite job?

What kind of job do you want to try?

You and me
being incredible

Date _____

Daughter, in 25 years, you'll be _____ years old.

If you remember just one thing
about who I am today, I hope it's

I predict you'll have more time to

You'll be really good at

For your birthday, you'll want

I'll probably give you

You'll still have to remind me to

We'll still be telling each other

Date _____

Mom, in 25 years, you'll be _____ years old.

If you remember just one thing
about who I am today, I hope it's

I predict you'll have more time to

You'll be really good at

For your birthday, you'll want

I'll probably give you

You'll still have to remind me to

We'll still be telling each other

Date _____

I have a question for you:

_____

_____

DEAR Daughter,

Do you think women are treated equal to men?

Is this topic important?

Do you think there are ways our society can improve?

Date _____

DEAR Mom,

What do you think about what I wrote
on men versus women?

Do you think men and women are treated equally?

How do you think our society can improve?

The view LOOKING OUT MY BEDROOM WINDOW

MOM

DAUGHTER

Date _____

YOU & ME

Date _____

DEAR Daughter

Hooray! We reached the end of our journal.
What did you like about writing together?

How should we celebrate our journal's completion?

What should we do with this journal?

Date _____

Celebrate your story

WITH THESE BELOVED PROMPT JOURNALS
BY KATIE CLEMONS

AWAITING YOU
Pregnancy journal

For the expecting mother yearning to celebrate the joy she's discovering as her heart expands and belly grows.

♡ I've kept this journal.
♡ I want this journal.
♡ I know _____ would love this!

BETWEEN MOM AND ME
Mother son journal

For the mother and son who crave a rule-free, creative way to connect with each other.

♡ I've kept this journal.
♡ I want this journal.
♡ I know _____ would love this!

TIME CAPSULE
A seriously awesome kid's journal

For the child who's curious to discover how mighty his own story can be.

♡ I've kept this journal.
♡ I want this journal.
♡ I know _____ would love this!

MONTANA
Travel journal

For the adventurer ready to assemble the perfect Big Sky State souvenir ... your story!

♡ I've kept this journal.
♡ I want this journal.
♡ I know _____ would love this!

Available online at https://katieclemons.com

CPSIA information can be obtained
at www.ICGtesting.com
Printed in the USA
LVOW10s2112131117
556087LV00008BA/398/P